# 射中！我們一起玩！

# Goal! Let's Play!

Joe Marriott
Illustrated by Algy Craig Hall

Chinese translation by Sylvia Denham

Mantra Lingua

我是阿振，
我每天都踢足球。

I'm Chen and I play football every day.

Thwack

boing

Goal!

Let's score!

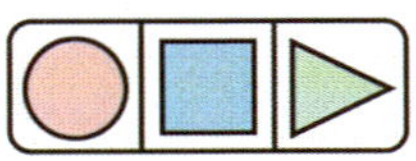

我的名字是丹尼雅娜，
我喜歡跟我的朋友
打籃球。

My name's Daniella.
I love playing basketball
with my friends.

**Boing**
**phwoop**
**through the hoop!**

**Let's shoot!**

我是阿查，我喜歡跟我的團隊打棒球。

I'm Chet and I love playing baseball with my team.

WHACK WHIZ

LET'S CATCH!

THUNK CAUGHT!

5 4

我的名字是花妮絲，爸爸
和我正在騎著駱駝競賽。

My name's Faris. Daddy and I are racing on a camel.

Humpety!

Bumpety!

Thumpety!

Let's ride!

我是卡蒂，
我在山頂放風箏。

I'm Katy and I fly my kite
at the top of the hill.

Let's fly!

Whoosh!

zoom!

Zip!

我的名字是皮亞，我是
全班中最快的跑手。

My name's Pierre. I'm the
fastest runner in my class.

**Huff puff whiz whistle!**

**Let's race!**

我是娜蒂亞，我喜歡與朋友
在水中游泳。

I'm Nadia and I love
swimming with my friends
in the cool water.

splish
splash
sploosh!

**Let's dive!**

我的名字是占姆士，我每個週末都和家人打網球。

My name's James.
I play tennis with my family every weekend.

**Whack!**

**Wham!**

***Boing!***

SLAM!

**Let's serve!**

我是瑪達，我正在
體育館内學柔道。

I’m Marta and I’m
learning judo in the gym.

**Spin!**

**Chop!**

**Flip!**

**Flop!**

**Let's throw!**

我是唐馬士，
我可以快速地滑雪。

I'm Tomas and I can ski
really fast.

*Swish! Swerve!*
*Whiiiiiiiiiiiiiiiiizzzzzzzz z z z!*

*Let's ski!*

我是尼迪舒，我喜歡跟朋友
和家人玩板球。

I'm Nitesh and I love playing
cricket with my friends and family.

Whoooosh!

Thwaaacc c c ckk!

Let's bowl!

Mexico
UK
Nigeria
Switzerland
Dubai
China
Australia
Indi
Spain
America
France